Heroes of the Day

The War on Terrorism

By Nancy Louis

Visit us at
www.abdopub.com

Published by ABDO Publishing Company, 4940 Viking Drive, Suite 622, Edina, Minnesota 55435. Copyright ©2002 by Abdo Consulting Group, Inc., Pentagon Tower, P.O. Box 36036, Minneapolis, Minnesota 55435 USA. International copyrights reserved in all countries. No part of this book may be reproduced in any form without written permission from the publisher.

Published 2002
Printed in the United States of America
Third printing 2003

Edited by Paul Joseph
Graphic Design: John Hamilton
Cover Design: Mighty Media
Photos: AP/Wide World, FEMA

Library of Congress Cataloging-in-Publication Data

Louis, Nancy, 1952-
    Heroes of the day / Nancy Louis.
        p. cm. — (War on terrorism)
    Includes index.
    Summary: Describes the actions of emergency telephone operators, police officers, firefighters, trained dogs, and individual citizens who helped in the aftermath of the terrorist attacks on the World Trade Center and Pentagon on September 11, 2001.
    ISBN 1-57765-658-X
    1. September 11 Terrorist Attacks, 2001—Juvenile literature. 2. Emergency management—United States—Juvenile literature. 3. Heroes—United States—Juvenile literature. [1. September 11 Terrorist Attacks, 2001. 2. Emergency management 3. Heroes]
I. Title. II. Series.

    HV6432.L68 2002
    363.34'97—dc21

                                             2001056066

Table of Contents

Heroes Among the Ruins

Rescue workers sift through the rubble of the World Trade Center.

Day of Heroes

S EPTEMBER 11, 2001, BEGAN AS AN ORDINARY day for most Americans. Children got ready for school. Adults left for work as businesses prepared to open. Then, at about 8:45 A.M., American Airlines Flight 11 slammed into the North Tower of the World Trade Center (WTC) in New York City. The explosion set the tower on fire about one-third of the way from the top. When American Airlines Flight 175 flew into the South Tower 18 minutes later, people realized it was no accident—it was a terrorist attack. Then, at 9:43 A.M., American Airlines Flight 77 crashed into the Pentagon. A fourth plane, United Airlines Flight 93, slammed into a field in Pennsylvania at 9:50 A.M. America was under attack.

It seemed unimaginable that the WTC towers would collapse, or that the Pentagon could be seriously damaged. Police officers, firefighters, rescue workers, emergency medical personnel, doctors, nurses, and 911 operators responded quickly and professionally to save as many lives as possible.

Thousands of ordinary people came to the aid of others on this tragic day, and in the weeks that followed. Many died trying to save those in need. Many others survived to recount the day's horrible events. September 11, 2001, will go down as a day of terror, and yet it was also a day of heroism.

WTC in Flames

Both towers of the World Trade Center burn after being struck by hijacked jetliners.

All-Out Emergency

ACROSS THE COUNTRY, 911 OPERATORS received phone calls. These calls later helped officials determine the sequence of events on September 11, 2001. The operators in the New York City area took calls from people who witnessed the plane crashes at the World Trade Center. The 911 operators dispatched police and firefighters to the scene, which quickly became a five-alarm call for help.

High-rise fires are normally very dangerous and hard to control, but these plane crashes caused especially intense explosions. Rescue workers expected many people to be seriously burned. Area hospitals were alerted to the critical situation. All emergency vehicles were called to the WTC to transport injured people to hospitals as quickly as possible.

Some emergency operators also took calls from people inside the stricken buildings. Some people called from their office phones or their cellular phones. The 911 operators instructed people to follow normal emergency procedures. These emergency operators were responsible for saving thousands of lives by their calmness and readiness in the face of extreme crisis.

Other 911 operators took calls from the passengers aboard the doomed flights. They heard firsthand accounts of the hijacking and an attempt to overtake the terrorists on United Airlines Flight 93.

The nation's 911 operators are trained to act rationally and professionally. Their role is to tell callers how to best handle their emergency and how to get appropriate help. These operators went beyond the call of duty on September 11, 2001, in a nationwide emergency.

911 Emergency

A 911 operator answers a call and dispatches aid through her computer.

Running in Fear

People flee for their lives as the South Tower of the World Trade Center collapses.

A Shower of Rubble

Police officers and civilians run in terror as one of the World Trade Center towers collapses.

NYPD Faces Tragedy

THE MEMBERS OF THE NEW YORK POLICE Department (NYPD) are highly trained, dedicated, and committed to service. The police officers enforce the laws, preserve the peace, reduce fear, and provide for a safe environment.

As the World Trade Center burned uncontrollably, all police departments rushed to the scene. Countless stories tell of heroic efforts from the NYPD and their brotherhood from surrounding areas and across the country. Approximately 60 members of local police departments are now listed as dead or missing.

On September 20, 2001, President George W. Bush recognized several members of the police department, including William Fischer and Padraig Carroll, in a speech to Congress. Officer William Fischer, a 16-year veteran of the NYPD and a member of the Emergency Service Unit, worked for over 17 straight days at the scene.

11

At the time of the disaster, Fischer was off duty. But he raced to the scene to rescue victims from the WTC rubble. Officer Padraig Carroll, an eight-year veteran of the New York Port Authority Police Department, was working at the WTC at the time of the attack. He, too, rushed to help in rescue operations at Ground Zero.

President Bush carries shield No. 1012 of another hero, New York Port Authority Police Officer George Howard. Bush carries this shield as a reminder of his responsibility to fight terrorism. Officer Howard worked for the police department for 16 years. He earned many medals and awards during those years, but he never bragged about his accomplishments. He loved his job. He rescued an elevator full of children in the World Trade Center bombing of 1993.

Though it was his day off, Howard rushed to the scene of the September 11 WTC disaster to help with the rescue mission. Howard was killed when the second tower collapsed.

Chaos in the Streets

Police try to direct traffic and pedestrians after the first WTC tower is struck.

Other stories of heroism include a group of 37 Norfolk, Virginia, police officers who gave up their vacation time to help their exhausted colleagues in New York. They assisted in the recovery of bodies, especially those of fallen police officers and firefighters. They also aided in discovering two firemen in the wreckage.

Honoring Fallen Heroes

President George W. Bush holds up the police shield of New York Police Officer George Howard, who died trying to save others in the World Trade Center.

Amidst the Ruins

New York City firefighter
looks up at what remains of
the collapsed World Trade
Center after the terrorist
attack September 11, 2001.

Firefighters Rise to the Challenge

FIREFIGHTERS ARE OFTEN THOUGHT OF AS heroes. But on September 11, 2001, the New York Fire Department (FDNY) showed extra bravery and courage. Every day, these firefighters put their lives on the line battling flames and saving lives. They know each other very well. Many live in the same neighborhoods. They tend to come from generations of firefighters. They say it's in their blood.

Squad 18, an elite rescue unit, was the very first department on the scene of the World Trade Center attack. According to survivors, Squad 18 climbed up the stairs in the North Tower as people frantically rushed down. Members of Squad 18 knew they had to keep going up as quickly as they could. They were fearful but they had a job to do, explained Gary Moore, one of the surviving firefighters from the squad. No one knows how far up the tower they climbed, but since they were the first on the scene, they probably were fairly high when it fell. All seven men on duty lost their lives.

Captain Patrick Brown and 11 members of Ladder Company 3 rushed up the stairs of the North Tower. Around the 35th floor, they radioed that 30 people were badly burned. A few minutes later, they yelled "Mayday!" The tower then collapsed. That was the last heard from these 12 men, who made up almost half of the department.

Daniel Nigro, a 32-year veteran and son of a fireman, was named the new chief of the New York Fire Department after his best friend and comrade, Chief of Department Peter Ganci, died at the World Trade Center. On the morning of September 11, both men were sitting in the fire station when they heard a crash

Searching the Rubble

Firefighters and rescue workers comb through the rubble of the World Trade Center, searching for survivors.

and then saw fire billowing from the tower. They drove together, heading across the Brooklyn Bridge toward the fire. Nigro said to Ganci that he thought this would be the worst day they would ever encounter.

Nigro manned the command center near the World Trade Center. Chief Ganci stayed with the rescuers and survived the collapse of the first tower. He moved to an area that put him in extreme danger. After the second tower fell, he was never seen again. He died doing what he did best, helping others in trouble.

The Reverend Mychal Judge, chaplain of FDNY, had taken off his hard hat to administer last rites to a fallen fireman, Deputy Chief Bill Feehan, when wreckage from the South Tower hit and killed him. Judge's parents immigrated from Ireland. His father died when he was six years old. At 14, he began his religious career by entering the seminary. Father Mike always wore the big, baggy brown habit of a monk. He was well-known for promoting peace in Northern Ireland, conducting masses for players at Yankee Stadium, and visiting the White House. He did these tasks along with his other daily duties, which included accompanying firefighters on call.

A memorial to Reverend Mychal Judge, the New York City Fire Department chaplain who died in the World Trade Center collapse.

Many firefighters and police live in the middle-class suburbs close to downtown New York City. They live and work together and consider each other family. As a young boy growing up in Franklin Square (a suburb on Long Island), Mike Kiefer dreamed of fighting fires in the big city. At 25, Mike joined the FDNY in December 2000. He was called "Mike the Keeper" by the other men in his unit, Ladder 132. They wanted him to stay when his probationary period expired at the end of October. He was at the firehouse when the emergency call came. All firefighters and equipment were needed immediately at the WTC. Mike and the Ladder 132 unit disappeared up the stairs of the South Tower and were never seen again.

President Bush recognized Battalion Chief John A. Jonas, a 21-year veteran of the FDNY. He and his men in Company 6 were one of the first rescue teams at the WTC. His company was buried in debris when the North Tower fell. Three hours later, they were rescued.

The New York Fire Department is missing 343 firefighters of its 13,000 members. Besides rebuilding the World Trade Center, New York must now rebuild its fire department.

A firefighter looking for trapped victims inside the World Trade Center makes his way up a stairwell crowded with people escaping to ground level.

Hazardous Duty

An unidentified firefighter tries to clear his eyes of soot during rescue efforts at the World Trade Center site.

To the Rescue

Deputy U.S. Marshal Dominic Guadagnoli helps an injured woman at the World Trade Center site.

Heroes to the Rescue

RESCUE SQUADS AND EMERGENCY MEDICAL personnel are trained to handle just about anything. Most of these workers cope by focusing on their jobs and working 12- to 20-hour shifts. Rescue teams from across the U.S. worked two-week shifts to relieve and support New York and help its recovery efforts.

Many survivors shared their stories in an attempt to restore their emotional state. Some are experiencing survivor's guilt. Some believe they are somehow responsible for sending others to the disaster and losing their lives. Others feel guilty for being off duty that day, which spared their lives.

Dr. Stephen Pierrel, director of psychological services for the Houston Fire Department, came with Houston volunteers to help rescuers deal with their personal reactions and emotions.

Les Dixon, an ER doctor from Utah, is part of a 62-member, four-dog Utah Task Force in New York City. Dixon staffs an on-site field hospital to handle rescue workers' minor injuries, such as scrapes, puncture wounds, headaches, and blisters.

A high school near the WTC was evacuated and set up as a triage center. Triage doctors, nurses, or paramedics examine injured people to determine the extent of their injuries. They treat minor injuries and send the others to hospitals or emergency rooms. On September 11, this makeshift center was ready to attend to hundreds of people, but very few arrived. Instead, the volunteers treated rescue workers with minor bumps and scrapes. They also washed ash out of the rescue workers' eyes while they drank coffee, ate cafeteria food, and told stories about the tragic day.

Racing Against Time

Rescue workers dig through the rubble of the WTC in search of trapped victims.

Helping Hands

Paramedics wash soot from the eyes of an injured rescue worker.

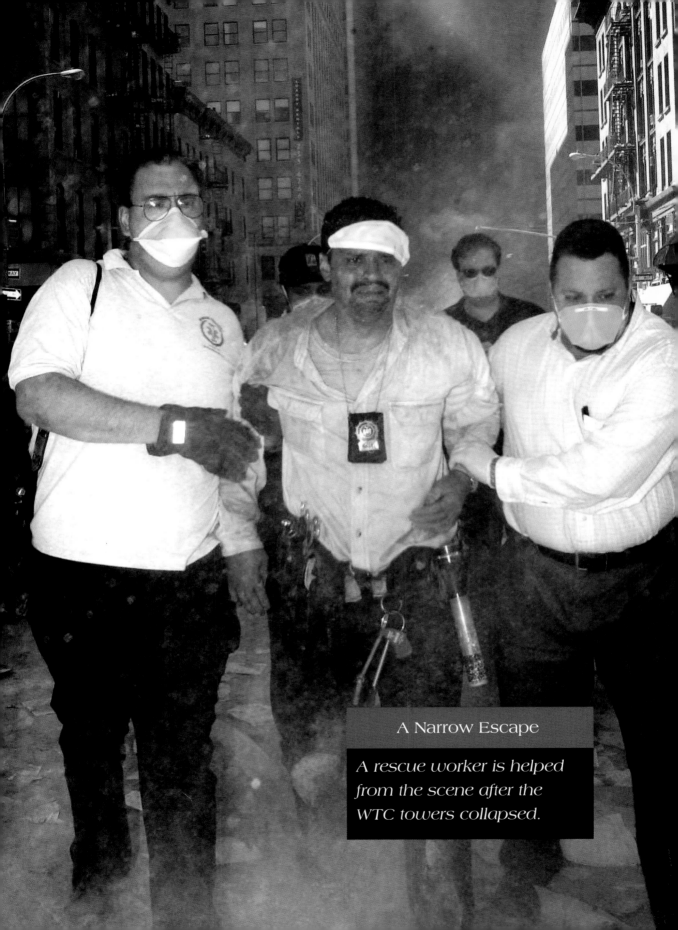

A Narrow Escape

A rescue worker is helped from the scene after the WTC towers collapsed.

Courage in the Chaos

MICHAEL BENFANTE AND JOHN CIQUEIRA worked in a telecommunications company on the 81st floor of the North Tower of the World Trade Center. When the first plane hit, Benfante told his employees to leave the building. As Benfante and Ciqueira reached the 68th floor of the stairwell, they saw a woman in a wheelchair. They carried her down to the 20th floor where firefighters offered to help. They knew the firefighters had so much to do, so they carried the woman the rest of the way down to safety and to a waiting ambulance. Everyone in Benfante's office miraculously made it out alive.

Zubair Munshey, 23, a Muslim of Pakistani descent living in Michigan, was attending a training seminar for a brokerage company in the South Tower of the WTC. When the first plane hit the North Tower, Munshey rushed to his building's 61st floor stairwell. At about the 20th floor, someone with a megaphone was shouting that everything was under control and that everyone should go back to their offices. But Munshey kept going down the stairs.

When he reached the bottom floor and ran out the door, the second plane hit the tower he had just come out of. He was screaming an Islamic prayer over and over, "There is no god worthy of worship but Allah, and Muhammad is his messenger." Thinking back about the day, he fears that people probably thought he was a terrorist.

Munshey walked to his hotel about six miles (10 km) from the WTC. It took him three hours to contact his parents in Michigan. They were relieved to hear he was alive, but they worried for his safety since he is a Muslim.

Munshey is worried about his life, too. He knows some Americans will hate him just because he is Muslim. Surviving the collapse of the WTC has made him resolve to make every day count, to read the Koran more often, and to be more conscious about saying unkind things about others.

A Blizzard of Debris

People in downtown Manhattan flee from the collapse of the WTC buildings.

Walking Wounded

People make their way out of the debris after the collapse of the World Trade Center towers.

Canine Rescue Team

John Randall poses with his dog Gunner. They spent a week searching the rubble of the World Trade Center.

Four-Legged Heroes

SHORTLY AFTER THE SEPTEMBER 11 ATTACK, about 350 specialty dogs, trained to find humans, worked in 12-hour shifts at the World Trade Center site. With names like Dutch, Tuff, Bigfoot, Sally, Porkchop, Max, and Cowboy, they tunneled through the twisted metal and rubble looking for signs of life. The dogs' handlers were members of fire or police departments, or were emergency medical technicians. They came from as far away as Europe. Most have worked at other disasters such as earthquakes, explosions, and accidents.

Cara, a two-year-old herding dog, had a camera strapped to her as she tunneled through areas to aid in rescuing people. Cholo, a German Shepherd from Texas, is part of an urban search and rescue crew who looks for survivors.

These dogs are trained to keep their legs spread when things move under their feet instead of jumping off the rubble. They learn to crouch in order to keep their balance when rubble shifts. They must be unflustered by people screaming and loud equipment. These dogs even learn how to climb ladders.

At the WTC, the dogs worked in teams in different parts of the wreckage. Before the dogs began to work, structural engineers investigated areas to determine how safe they were to explore. Hazardous-materials specialists first looked for dangerous substances such as jet fuel, diesel fuel, or Freon. Then the dogs were sent in. When they found something, they either barked or laid down at the spot. Then rescue specialists came to see what the dogs had found.

The Veterinary Assistance Medical Team (VAMT), composed of volunteer men and women and veterinarians, staffed a medical station a few blocks from the WTC ruins. They examined the dogs before they started their rescue missions. When the dogs returned after their shifts, many were treated for cut foot pads, ear and eye cleaning, exposure to chemicals, and dehydration. Then the dogs were bathed, fed, and sent to rest areas, where they played with donated toys and bones until their next shift began.

Team Players

A search and rescue canine team from France helps out at the WTC site.

Eager to Help

Mary Flood leashes Jake, her black Labrador retriever, before searching through the ruins of the WTC.

Direct Hit on the Pentagon

Officer Randy Lazzato watches as firefighters work to put out the flames at the Pentagon.

Pentagon Under Attack

AS THE HORROR AT THE WORLD TRADE Center unfolded, a third hijacked jetliner slammed into the Pentagon in Washington, D.C. The Pentagon was thought to be the safest, most secure building in the world. Yet it suffered substantial damage in one section. The plane's impact caused a huge explosion, with intense fire and smoke.

Army Lieutenant Colonel Victor Correa was knocked to the floor by the impact. He knew he had to get up and help people leave the building. Years of military training prepared him and others for this emergency. He covered his face with a wet shirt and told dazed workers to follow his voice through the smoke to safety. Correa then went back inside and broke down fire doors to rescue more office workers.

Army Sergeant Major Tony Rose heard cries for help coming from a huge pile of debris. He organized a tunnel-digging team that rescued seven trapped workers.

Lieutenant Colonel Sean Kelly and Captain Darrell Oliver lifted a desk off a secretary. Oliver carried her out of the building on his back. Oliver then went back into the same area. He rescued a deaf janitor who was crying hysterically. Oliver calmed the man as he carried him out of the fallen debris.

Navy Seaman First Class Cean Whitmarsh was watching the disaster at the World Trade Center on the television in his Pentagon office. Suddenly the building shook, windows blew out, and the ceiling fell on him and his co-workers. He knew then that the Pentagon had been attacked. Whitmarsh put his emergency training to work and organized a team that cut through a fence toward the center of the crash and pulled people to safety.

Thousands of people were running toward exits as Navy captain Dr. Stephen Frost ran straight into the thick black smoke. He was one of the first on the scene, helping traumatized and badly burned victims. He and Captain John Feerick, another Navy doctor, worked until dark treating the injured and stabilizing patients on the lawn of the Pentagon. That night they slept on the concrete with a blanket until the Red Cross brought tents and cots.

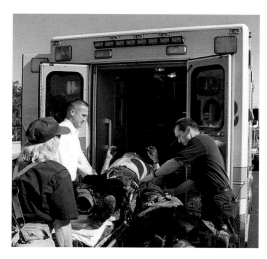

An injured person from the Pentagon is loaded into an ambulance outside the building.

Comforting the Wounded

A Pentagon employee is aided after escaping the burning building.

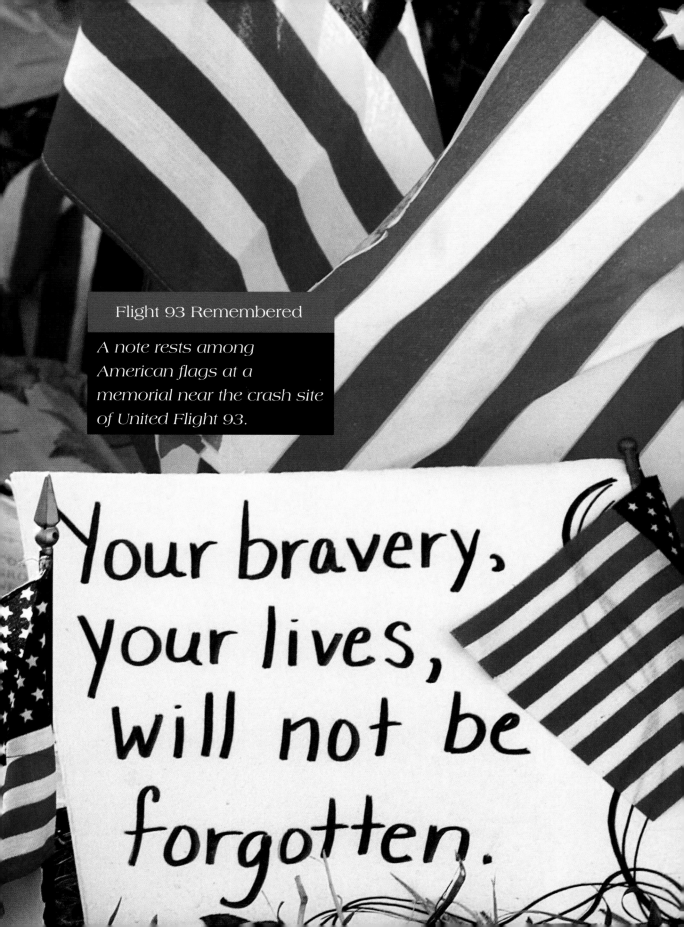

Flight 93 Remembered

A note rests among American flags at a memorial near the crash site of United Flight 93.

Your bravery, your lives, will not be forgotten.

Fighting Back on Flight 93

AFTER THE WORLD TRADE CENTER AND Pentagon attacks, there was fear of another hijacking as United Airlines Flight 93 veered off course, heading toward Washington, D.C. But at 10:37 a.m. the plane fell from the sky, crashing into a farm field near Shanksville, Pennsylvania, southeast of Pittsburgh.

Much more is known about what happened on Flight 93 than the other hijackings. There was more communication between the passengers, 911 operators, and family members. It is believed that several brave passengers decided to take back control of the plane from the terrorists. The plane crashed after a wild and violent struggle. All of the passengers and crew died in the crash.

Before the crash, passenger Jeremy Glick called his wife and in-laws in New York from the air phone on the hijacked plane. His mother-in law called the state police on another phone while Glick was still on the line and relayed information about the hijacking. Glick described the hijackers as three Arabs. One of the hijackers had a red box he said was a bomb. Another had a knife.

Passengers Mark Bingham, Tom Burnett, and Todd Beamer heroically jumped the hijackers. They knew the World Trade Center had been attacked, and that their own hijacked plane would probably be used to kill more innocent people on the ground. Bingham, Burnett, and Beamer knew they had to do something to stop the terrorists. They were willing to die to save others.

Later, U.S. Senator John McCain honored Mark Bingham at his memorial service as one of the Americans who lost his life trying to stop terrorism. Mark Bingham is remembered as a hard-working and fun-loving man who loved life.

Tom Burnett made four calls to his wife in California before the plane crashed. She said her husband thought he was going to solve the problem and that he would be home that night.

Moments before the plane crashed, Todd Beamer called 911 and spoke to operator Lisa Jefferson. He said he thought the pilot and co-pilot were fatally injured and that two of the hijackers were flying the plane while a third was guarding the passengers. He said he knew they were not going to survive. Beamer asked the operator to pray with him and then asked her to call his wife and tell her he loved her. He left his phone on while he joined the others as they stormed the terrorists in an attempt to thwart the hijacking plot. His last words were, "Are you ready? Let's roll!" Todd's wife, Lisa, who was expecting their third child, says she has so many things she will tell their children about their father—his courage, his character, his faith, his integrity, and his love of his family. His story, along with those of others who gave their lives to save others, will give her strength through the difficult times ahead.

Captain of Doomed Flight 93

Sheryl Stoll holds a photo of her cousin, Captain Jason Dahl, who was killed when Flight 93 was hijacked.

Presidential Praise

President Bush puts his arm around firefighter Bob Beckwith while touring the devastation of the WTC site.

Honoring the Heroes

NOTHING CAN REPLACE THOSE WHO LOST their lives on September 11, 2001. To honor these brave heroes, military and civilian medals are being awarded for extraordinary service. Secretary of Defense Donald Rumsfeld announced that armed forces personnel who died in the attack will receive the Purple Heart military decoration. The Purple Heart is a combat medal, but President Bush declared the attack on America "not just acts of terror, but an act of war."

Civilian Defense Department employees who were killed or wounded in the attacks will receive a newly created decoration, the Defense of Freedom medal. Non-Defense Department personnel may also be awarded this medal.

The front of the gold, round medal has the phrase "Defense of Freedom" framing a bald eagle holding a shield. It represents the principles of freedom and the defense of those freedoms that the United States stands for. The back of the medal is inscribed with the words, "On behalf of a grateful nation," with a space for the recipient's name. A wreath of leaves represents honor and high achievement.

The medal has a red, white, and blue ribbon. The red stripes stand for valor and sacrifice. There are four red stripes. Each stripe represents one of the attacks made with a hijacked plane. The wide blue stripe represents the attack on the Pentagon. The white stripes symbolize liberty as represented on the American flag.

Hundreds of memorial services, prayer services, moments of silence, and candlelight vigils around the world remember those who gave their lives in the name of freedom. It is estimated that 62 nations experienced loss of life from these attacks. The final toll of casualties may never be known.

Defense of Freedom Medal

OBVERSE   **REVERSE**

September 11, 2001, will go down in history as a day of tragedy and triumph as everyday heroes came together, helped others, and refused to be defeated by terrorism.

A Tribute to Heroes

A child hands a New York City firefighter a flower to place on a memorial in the rubble of the World Trade Center.

Timeline

8:45 A.M.   American Airlines Flight 11 crashes into the North Tower of the World Trade Center, setting it on fire.

9:03 A.M.   United Airlines Flight 175 slams into the South Tower of the World Trade Center, setting it on fire as well.

9:30 A.M.   President George W. Bush announces that the nation has suffered a terrorist attack.

9:40 A.M.   The Federal Aviation Administration halts all flight operations at all U.S. airports.

9:43 A.M.   American Airlines Flight 77 crashes into the Pentagon.

10:05 A.M.   The South Tower of the World Trade Center collapses.

10:10 A.M.   A portion of the Pentagon collapses.

10:28 A.M.   The North Tower of the World Trade Center collapses.

10:48 A.M.   Police confirm the crash of United Flight 93 in Pennsylvania.

11:02 A.M.   New York Mayor Rudolph Giuliani asks New Yorkers to stay home and orders everyone south of Canal Street to leave the area.

1:04 P.M.   President Bush promises the U.S. will find and punish the people responsible for the attacks.

1:44 P.M.   Aircraft carriers USS *George Washington* and USS *John F. Kennedy* along with five warships leave Norfolk, Virginia, for the New York coast to further protect the area.

4:00 P.M.   U.S. officials say they believe Osama bin Laden is connected to the attacks.

5:20 P.M.   The 47-story Building 7 of the World Trade Center collapses.

7:45 P.M.   New York officials report that nearly 80 police officers and up to 200 firefighters are believed to have been killed during rescue operations.

8:30 P.M.   President Bush addresses the nation.

Where on the Web?

http://www.people.com

In the search box, type "attack on America and heroes" or "World Trade Center and heroes" to find stories about everyday heroes from the disaster on September 11, 2001.

http://teacher.scholastic.com/newszone/specialreports/ under_attack/kids_help.htm

"Kids Make a Difference," a special online issue from Scholastic.

http://www.ci.nyc.ny.us/html/fdny/home.html

The official Fire Department, City of New York (FDNY) web site.

http://www.ci.nyc.ny.us/html/nypd/home.html

Official site of the New York Police Department.

http://www.fema.gov/usr/usr_canines.htm

Canine Rescue: From the Federal Emergency Management Agency (FEMA), this web site explains the canine's role in search-and-rescue efforts. Includes photos and a special kids' page.

Glossary

brotherhood

An association for a particular purpose; a whole group of persons engaged in the same profession. Firefighters and police departments consider themselves members of the same brotherhood and sisterhood.

casualty

A person who is injured or killed in an act of war.

colleagues

People connected by being in the same profession or office.

descent

Being of a specific background, culture, and heritage from a specific country.

five-alarm fire

The largest and most dangerous call for help that involves fire department emergency assistance from many stations.

ground zero

The point directly above, below, or at which an explosion occurs. As the first tower collapsed, the World Trade Center was instantly referred to as "Ground Zero."

heroism

Acts of great courage, high achievement, and noble qualities that bring to mind extreme adoration and devotion.

hijack

To take over an airplane by force.

mayday

An international radio-telephone signal word used as an emergency distress call.

memorial

Something that keeps remembrance alive. After the World Trade Center disaster, many memorials around the world commemorated those who died.

plot

A secret plan for accomplishing a usually evil or unlawful deed.

terrorism

A systematic use of terror as a means to harm or scare others who do not hold true the same political, religious, or cultural practices and beliefs.

triage

The sorting of patients and what kind of treatment they need by prioritizing their injuries to save as many people as possible from a disaster.

Index